The Date Book

A Teen Girl's Complete Guide to Going Out With Someone New

By Erika Stalder

Illustrated by Helen Dardik

First published in 2007 by
Zest Books, an imprint of Orange Avenue Publishing
35 Stillman Street, Suite 121, San Francisco, CA 94107
www.zestbooks.net

Created and produced by Zest Books, San Francisco, CA
© 2007 by Orange Avenue Publishing LLC
Illustrations © 2007 by Helen Dardik

Text set in Filosofia; title and accent text set in Imperfect

Library of Congress Control Number: 2007925697
ISBN-13: 978-0-9772660-8-1
ISBN-10: 0-9772660-8-7

CREDITS
EDITORIAL DIRECTOR: Karen Macklin
CREATIVE DIRECTOR: Hallie Warshaw
WRITER: Erika Stalder
EDITOR: Karen Macklin
ILLUSTRATOR: Helen Dardik
GRAPHIC DESIGNER: Cari McLaughlin
PRODUCTION ARTIST: Cari McLaughlin

Printed in China.
First printing, 2007
10 9 8 7 6 5 4 3 2 1

*Every effort has been made to ensure that the information presented is accurate. Readers
are strongly advised to read product labels, follow manufacturers' instructions, and heed
warnings. The publisher disclaims any liability for injuries, losses, untoward results, or
any other damages that may result from the use of the information in this book.*

The Date Book

Going out with someone new

can be the most exhilaratingly sweet rush ever. You get an exclusive opportunity to give attention to — and get attention from — that hottie you've been thinking about so much.

From the jump, it all seems great. You fantasize about being your fierce, darling, witty, super-fun self — always saying the right thing at the right time and looking fabulous while doing it. The first-date fantasy is sooo working for you.

But then, the questions start rushing in: How am I going to get my hypersensitive parents to let me out? What am I going to wear? Where are we gonna go? And ... is it even a date?

Clearly, there's a lot to handle.

But don't worry. It's actually a lot simpler than it seems. And though dating is completely and wholly unpredictable, you *can* prep yourself.

In *The Date Book*, you'll learn all the dating dirt they don't teach in school, like how to read confusing signals from guys, persuade strict parents to let you go out, avoid creeps, and create physical boundaries without feeling like a total prude. You'll do self-analysis to find out **what type of first date outing works best for you**, what your motives are for going out with someone new, and how you can get ready in 10 minutes flat for an impromptu rendezvous (yes, it can be done). *The Date Book* is also chock-full of advice on what to say, how to act, and how to exit if your dream dude turns out to be a total dud.

We've navigated the treacherous dating waters and interviewed dozens of high school boys for this book (after all, you don't know what they're thinking unless you ask, right?) to be able to give you **the complete lowdown** on everything you need to know. This way, when it comes time for the big day with your new guy, you can relax, carry yourself with confidence, and have a great time — after all, that's the point, isn't it?

Table of Contents

1 Dating DNA:
What Makes a Date?
9

2 Activate Your Date:
Letting Him Know You're Interested
25

3 Figuring Out the 411:
Where to Go and What to Do
37

4 You vs. the People Who (Try to) Run Your Life:
Surefire Strategies for Winning Parental Approval
47

5 Date Expectations:
Writing a Dating Contract and Spotting Red Flags
59

6 Lights, Wardrobe ... Action!

Creating the Perfect Look
for Your Date

71

7 Readying Your Bod, Your
Bag, and Your Brain:

Recipes for Panic-Free Prepping

85

8 That Did *Not*
Just Happen:

Coping With Date-Related
Embarrassment

95

9 Make Out or Make
Your Escape:

How to Sweeten or
Shorten Your Date

103

10 Afterglow or Aftermath?

Getting (or Avoiding) That
Second Date

111

1 Dating DNA:

What Makes a Date?

What Exactly Comprises a Date?

As with the words *love* and *like*, the term
dating is subjective and can be defined
thousands of different ways. Understanding
what a date is — and if you are on one — can be
harder than stacking a complete Jenga tower
while wearing mittens.

Throughout time, the double helix of dating has mystified
many. Consider the most famous of young lovers, Romeo
and Juliet. One could argue that the pair never, in fact,
dated. They met at a party, got married the next day, and the
next time they rendezvoused, it was for their own funerals.
Audrey Hepburn's character in *Breakfast at Tiffany's* hung
out with many men. Was she technically dating ALL of
them? Or were they just "seeing each other," "going out,"
or none of the above? And then there are the two characters
in *When Harry Met Sally*. They developed their friendship
over decades by going to restaurants, museums, and
parties, yet refused to classify their excursions as
dates — only to end up together after all.

So, what exactly is a date? Is your after-school ice cream
run with the hottie from fourth period a date? Or simply a
way to handle your simultaneous sugar rushes? And what
about that football game where you met up with your crush

after making loose plans via text? You guys had a great time, but you're not sure what the next step is. How can you possibly know how to proceed?

Things have gotten even more confusing over the past few decades. We hear about the wonderfully clear-cut days of Johnny asking Betty to the drive-in, but those type of dates are now as rare as drive-ins themselves. In today's world, girls and guys are seen more as equals and hang out as friends all the time. This certainly has its advantages, but it leaves room for lots of ambiguity—and sometimes a girl needs to play detective to figure out whether an outing is date-ish or just friend-ly.

Playing Sleuth

When trying to ascertain whether or not you are actually on a date, it's important to look out for any context clues. Say you go to the movies together. Does he dress a little nicer than usual? Is he nervous, more polite, and sitting a little closer? Wearing cologne? If so, smells like a date. Does he show up in odorific sweats and spend the evening talking about some other girl? In that case, maybe not.

If he invites you to hang out in a group setting, the situation gets trickier. First, there's the factor that he didn't ask just YOU—he asked a whole bunch of people. Date or social outing? Second, he is spending his time with everyone. If you see him talking to another girl present, you might wonder if he's vibing *her*. Or if he bros out with a fellow music-obsessed dude and spends the evening yammering on about Clapton vs. Hendrix, 12-string vs. 6-string, and emo vs. indie, you might think they'd be better off dating each other.

To make your life easier, here's a little chart to help with interpreting those context clues the next time you're out and thinking: Is this a date?

Destination Datesville?	Oh Yeah	Not So Much
He personally asks you to go somewhere, then checks in later to make sure you're still going.	✦	
While out, he throws his arm around your shoulder when other guys approach, emitting the "she's with me" vibe.	✦	
He asks you to go out — and asks all of your friends along.		✦
He teases you — but not in a mean way.	✦	
While out, he talks to you about other girls.		✦
He doesn't put any attention into the way he dresses.		✦
If in a group, he makes sure he sits next to you on the Tilt-a-Whirl, in the movies, or at dinner.	✦	

Destination Datesville?	Oh Yeah	Not So Much
If in a group, he concentrates more on other people there.		⚛
He doesn't personally greet you or say good-bye when he arrives or leaves.		⚛
He finds an incog way to touch you, by playing footsie under the table or brushing up against you.	⚛	
He checks in with you throughout the evening to make sure you're having a good time.	⚛	
He sends lots of smiles straight your way.	⚛	
He pays more attention to his cell phone/PSP/pocketful of gadgets than to you.		⚛
He makes (casual) open invitations for future plans.	⚛	

If he's not sending out any signals, send a few yourself—like touching his arm when you talk to him or looking in his eyes while you flash your knock-'em-dead smile—and see what kind of response you get. The key is to be attentive to what's going on around you so you know where you stand.

What Type of Date Is Best for You?

Not sure what type of date jibes with your social style? Check out these pros and cons of different kinds of going-outings.

The One-on-One Date

The Pros:

- ❋ Exclusive time and devoted attention with your new guy
- ❋ Don't have to consult with others to make a plan
- ❋ Privacy

The Cons:

- ❋ All plan-making pressures are on you or him
- ❋ All conversation must be generated by the two of you
- ❋ No backup from buddies
- ❋ Greatest chance of resistance from the 'rents

The Double Date

The Pros:

- More mouths make it easier to break the ice
- Less pressure to make conversation
- You have a fellow girl to recap the night with

The Cons:

- Can get uncomfortable if the two people in the other couple don't get along well with each other
- Can get uncomfortable if the two people in the other couple get along *too* well with each other
- Not as much privacy

Rules for New Romance

Keep It Solo

Don't invite friends to barge in on a one-on-one date. If you feel you may need the support of friends while you're out, schedule a double date or group outing. Inviting a surprise third wheel betrays the exclusivity with which you agreed to go out.

The Blind Date

The Pros:

- ❈ All you have to do is show up

- ❈ Surprises are fun (he could be a gem)

- ❈ If it's a good setup, your date will be someone who shares your views and passions

The Cons:

- ❈ Can get set up with someone who's too insecure to bag his own date

- ❈ Surprises are not always fun (he could be a turd)

- ❈ If you decide you're not into him, it could affect your relationship with mutual friends

The Group Date

The Pros:

- ❋ The conversation rolls along with little effort

- ❋ Escape routes a plenty

- ❋ Help from your girls in reading his signals

- ❋ Getting permission from the 'rents? Cake.

The Cons:

- ❋ Common side effect: the wandering eye

- ❋ You're sharing your date with a dozen other friends

- ❋ Sneak-away make-out sessions can be tricky to orchestrate

What Kind of Dater Are You?

To find out what kind of date best suits your personality, take the following quiz.

1. My idea of a good time is:

   A. Ping-Pong, a trip around the Ferris wheel, or anything built for two … I like to give people my undivided attention, one homey at a time.

   B. a proper dinner with a few of my closest friends, dim lighting, and light music in the background.

   C. checking out a film I've never heard of at the foreign film house.

   D. a party, man—150 of my closest friends, catering, and a dance floor.

2. Making conversation is:

   A. a snap—as long as I can focus on one person and no one else buts in.

   B. like an old car—difficult to start, but fun once you get it going.

   C. best when you don't know someone at all and can exchange plenty of get-to-know-you questions.

   D. easy, breezy, beautiful.

3. I plan my own birthday parties:

A. by myself and 11 months in advance — every detail must be perfect.

B. every once in a while, but usually I like to just play it by ear.

C. never. It's cooler when other people plan it, invite a random crowd, and just ask me to show up.

D. ... plan? A venue full of people plus me equals insta-party.

4. When I walk into a room, I want:

A. the guy I have my eyes on to have his eyes on me — and no one else.

B. a few people to check my cute outfit.

C. to notice a fresh, new face in the crowd.

D. to talk to everyone in the room — all at once.

5. When prepping for a biology final I usually:

   A. host a three-hour cram session with my lab partner.

   B. meet up with a small study group of people I know.

   C. ask some people I've never met before to form a study group—what a great way to meet new people!

   D. meet up with as many study groups as I can—12 minds are better than one.

6. My favorite way of chatting is:

   A. face-to-face—all that other stuff is so superficial.

   B. in a familiar setting with a familiar crew (like catching up with teammates after soccer practice).

   C. striking up a random conversation with someone on the bus or in line at the grocery store.

   D. texting, IMing, emailing, three-way calling … do I have to choose?

7. If I were a *Sex in the City* character, I would be:

   A. Miranda

   B. Charlotte

   C. Carrie

   D. Samantha

Mostly As: Solo Dater

You're a quality over quantity girl. You prefer to devote your attention to one thing at a time and love to take control of the details. What some might consider a pressure situation—hanging out with a new person on your own—is a walk in the park for you. Solo dating is your best bet.

Mostly Bs: Double Dater

You date well with others. You love having a friend in tow to share your experiences and to let you know if you have lipstick on your teeth. Double-dating creates a perfect balance of hanging out in an intimate group without having to carry the burden of all conversation and decision-making.

Mostly Cs: Blind Dater

When it comes to dating, you are part romantic, part investigative reporter. You love meeting new people from all walks of life and trying to figure them out. You're not afraid to roll the emotional dice and appreciate the theory of having to kiss a lot of frogs before you meet your prince—which makes you the ultimate blind dater.

Mostly Ds: Group Dater

You're an assertive, know-what-you-want, attention-loving lady who excels at getting parties started and keeping them going. Group dating perfectly suits your more-the-merrier attitude and allows you to hit the party and have a date at the same time. Genius!

2 Activate Your Date:

Letting Him Know You're Interested

Getting the Ball Rolling

Let's face it: Boys aren't always as proactive, mature, or clued-in as the ladies. This is not said in the spirit of boy-bashing. Research has shown that girls develop social and organizational skills earlier than guys. And, as any girl who has towered over her partner during a junior high slow dance knows, the female body develops earlier as well. Of course, the menfolk have plenty of other things going for them: charm, playful spirits, humor, and deliciously built shoulders. But they can be pretty illiterate when it comes to reading between the lines.

The point is that sometimes it's up to the girls to initiate a date. There are two ways to do it. The Type A approach—for the outgoing mover and shaker who likes to make things happen—would be to simply ask a guy out; the Type B approach—for the reserved, shy, and introspective girl who doesn't like to take risks—is to drop hints and engage in mild flirtation until *he* does the asking. Both approaches are positive, proactive ways of letting a guy know you're interested in him and would like to go out sometime. Read them over and decide which one to use to snag your next first date.

The Type A Approach: Get Yours

In our poor foremothers' day, asking a guy out signified desperation. It also created social awkwardness. Women were supposed to be chased, not doing any chasing. Lucky for us, that ideology has been shed (along with ankle-length hemlines and imprisoning undergarments).

It's perfectly fine for a girl to ask a guy to a movie, and, what's more, the success rate is much higher than you might think. Of the dozens of guys interviewed for this book, the majority said they would say "yes" if a girl asked them out. Their logic: *Why not* go out with a girl who asks? And the few who wouldn't spit out a "yes"? They were more concerned with protecting their macho, player image. (Total red flag, BTW.) Bottom line: If he does say no, he's probably not the mature, smart, and savvy guy you want to spend your time with anyway.

The Philosophy: Why wait for life to happen to you when you can make things happen yourself?

The Inspiration: Madonna

The Execution: Though you might think you're up for the task (and you definitely are), even the gutsiest chicks get butterflies when push comes to shove. Here are tips for making your move without acting like a fool.

DIY. Don't send a friend to do your job. This not only comes across as immature, but also doesn't give him much incentive for saying yes. If you can't be bothered to ask him yourself, why should he bother to spend his time with you? Another potential glitch is that he may think it's your friend who actually likes him. The results of this equation are also potentially disastrous. If you're not secure enough to talk to him yourself, you shouldn't be asking.

Be direct. Asking a guy out via text, email, or even IM leaves the door open for a barrage of communication misfires:

   a. His email provider might not recognize your address and send your provoking, thoughtful, and perfectly crafted message straight to his spam folder.

   b. His wireless connection might disconnect right when you send your IM.

   c. Your text may take two days to go through.

For a girl who is going for what she wants, these methods leave too many chances for a breakdown (communication or otherwise).

By asking him in person — or even over the phone (make sure he's not totally preoccupied while you chat) — your proposal can't get warped within the time-space continuum that is modern-day communication.

Be specific. Boys understand subtlety about as much as they understand PMS. And you want a direct response, not something you'll have to spend the next two weeks dissecting with your five best friends. "I was wondering if you might like to hang out sometime" leaves you open to a vague answer like, "Yeah, um, sometime." Something more specific and direct like, "Wanna go to homecoming together?" or "I have an extra ticket to a death-rock show on Friday. Interested?" will enable him to provide a clear-cut yes or no response, so you won't have to wonder if he's into it.

Time it right. The best time to ask him out is when you can catch him alone, without his crew. He won't be tempted to pull the too-cool card under the influence of his ill-behaving posse and instead pay complete attention to you.

Keep things in perspective. Though asking him out feels like a big deal, do keep in mind the significance of this moment in regard to finishing high school (minimal), the impact this will have on your life as a whole (minute), and how this will affect the planet (nil).

Now that you've mentally cut this event down to size, you can do the deed with an air of nonchalance that will keep you sharp and the convo light and casual.

The Risks: Obviously, you're putting your (irresistible) butt on the line here. Dude could say no and you'll walk away embarrassed, bummed, or both. You may be tempted to speculate as to why he turned you down. Don't waste your time. The bottom line is it's not the end of the world. If he can't hang with your fabulous self, try setting your sights on someone new. And keep in mind, the more practice you have at asking guys out, the less it will bother you when they say no.

The Type B Approach: Protect Your Neck

It's only natural to be reserved about asking a guy out. But keeping your defenses up won't put you in the game. And you gotta be in it ... to win it. You *can* let a boy know you like him without totally going in for the kill. Playing nice, flirting, and hinting that you're available for kickage are all techniques that have been used for centuries to get the message across. Then he is perfectly positioned to do the asking (if he's interested), and you won't be taking the risk yourself. And if your guy is a bit traditional, he may appreciate being handed the reins.

The Philosophy: If you build it, he will come.

The Inspiration: Marilyn Monroe

The Execution: There's a fine line between stalking and suggesting. Here are some fail-proof ways to let him know you like him without coming across as a groupie.

Put him in your realm. Letting a guy know you like him without interaction is pretty impossible. To get him in the mix, invite him to parties or other functions your friends are having. If you invite him to a few events and he never shows, he's probably not interested.

Talk to him. There are millions of reasons for human interaction each day. Next time you stand next to him in the lunch line or share a shift with him at work, compliment him on his shirt or ask about his weekend. Flirt a bit. The more you converse, the more he'll notice and enjoy your positive attention.

Drop hints. Give him a chance to easily ask you out by letting him know what you like to do. If you'd love to go to the movies with him, tell him you can't wait to see the latest horror flick. This leaves the door wide open for an invitation.

Show your support. A great way to let a guy know you're interested in him is to take a special interest in his life. By showing up at his basketball game or helping him figure out that tricky geometry problem, you're not only slyly inserting yourself into his realm, but you're also proving you care without coming right out and saying it.

RULES for New ROMANCE

✷ Snagging Your Crush ✷

Holding his glance for a moment or two is a sweet flirting technique. In conversation, making eye contact not only exudes tremendous confidence, but also shows that you're actively listening. If he's at all a looker, this shouldn't be tough.

The Risks: Sometimes, even when you put something under someone's nose, they still don't smell what's going on. If he isn't picking up what you're throwing down, you may need to go for the more direct Type A approach. But proceed with caution: It's also possible that he's simply not interested. If this is the case, all the flirting and conversing will simply become annoying. If you notice he's becoming short with you, or not exactly reciprocating the love, cease fire and move on.

RULES for New ROMANCE

✳ Keep It Real ✳

If you've got his royal hot-ness perched on a pedestal, dethrone him immediately. No matter how ethereal he may seem, the dude takes his vitamins, brushes his teeth (hopefully), and kisses his mama the same way you do. The sooner you embrace his realness, the better. It's much easier to flirt with some-one you've mentally filed as "hot but attainable" than to approach someone you've categorized as a demigod. To stabilize your mental and biological giddiness the next time you see him in the hall, remind yourself that underneath that ripped, swimmer's body, he farts, has fears, and can be just as dorky as your BFF.

HIS ROYAL HOTNESS

3

Figuring Out the 411:

Where to Go and What to Do

Making Plans

If you're going to do the asking, you need to have a plan—
like where you're gonna go, when you're gonna roll, and all
that jazz. But even when you don't do the asking, it never
hurts to have a backup; unforeseen circumstances like
unruly weather and sold-out shows can make for awkard
last-minute decision-making. And just in case his plan
sucks, you'll have a fabulous Plan B already in the bag.

Classic Dates

A first date can be nerve-wracking enough without trying to
plan something extraordinary. If you want to keep the vibe
casual and the date simple, try a classic date. These tried-
and-true outings have gotten the job done for generations.

1. The Dinner

We all have to eat. When picking the location, look for a
restaurant that isn't too pricey. Since many guys do offer to
pay, picking the most expensive place in town is presump-
tuous and in poor taste, even if they do serve the finest
lobster. When considering cuisine, omit fare that will leave
you with the rank, unkissable breath that even the strongest
of mints won't fix (hello, garlic!) as well as foods like sushi,
spaghetti, and ribs, which can slip out of chopsticks, forks,
and fingers in a heartbeat.

When ordering, also keep in mind that few guys like a girl who pulls the malnourished starlet routine—picking her way through an undressed salad in lieu of an actual meal. That move just reeks of insecurity, which is hardly attractive and, worse, will leave you ravenously hungry.

The Perk: Sharing food—a great way to up the flirting ante.

Perfect for: The conversationalist. The time between ordering and when food arrives is just right for getting-to-know-you chat.

2. The Movie

Who doesn't like to be entertained? The movie is perhaps the most fail-proof first date because you both get to laugh, cry, and go on fantastic journeys without having to be particularly witty, emotionally available, or equipped for intergalactic travel.

Although you may be dying to see the new Reese Witherspoon flick, ask yourself if your guy seems like the romantic comedy-loving type. Or, better yet, ask *him*. If he's not down for tears and sappy love scenes, save it for a night with the girls and pick a film on more neutral territory.

The Perk: Built-in opportunities for cuddling in the dark without expectations of taking off any clothes.

Perfect for: The shy girl or nervous mess. Even in the worst of films, the characters on the screen do all the talking. What's more, the plotline (or lack thereof) gives you something to discuss later.

3. The School Dance

Despite the tacky decor, this date is loaded with classically romantic elements: dim lighting, slow jams, and formal attire. You get to rock that strapless dress you've been dying to wear without looking like you tried too hard. You also get to hang with plenty of other people—but when it comes time for the R&B jams, you've got a designated partner.

The Perk: Dancing cheek to cheek, of course.

Perfect for: The girl who loves tradition, elegance, and boys in suits—and who won't trip on the gaggle of gawking chaperones present.

4. The Party

This is a kind of noncommittal date. You get to show up with some delicious arm candy, but still dance with other people. The party date can be tricky to navigate. While it's important to give your guy autonomy and time to mingle on his own, don't forget you came with him. Be sure to check up on him from time to time and drag him out on the dance floor for some clean, flirty fun.

The Perk: You get to hang with your friends *and* steal away for marathon make-out sessions with your new dude.

Perfect for: The "it" girl who wants to have her cake and eat it, too.

A Date Less Ordinary

If you and your date aren't into mainstream stuff—like school dances, sporting events, parties, or whatever the rest of the kids are doing—try a more creative first date. This doesn't mean arranging for a private jet ride, a four-course meal on a boat, or any of those other fantastic, Hollywood-inspired date feats that take a multimillion-dollar budget (and a fictional story line) to pull off. Lack of cash flow or green screen technology shouldn't stop you from arranging an off-the-hook first date. Try one of these affordable ideas—or make up one of your own.

1. Take and Give Lessons

You and your guy might not know much about each other on your first date. A surefire way to accelerate the getting-to-know-you period is to offer to teach him about one of your passions or learn more about one of his. If you're an expert on horseback, offer to take him out for a ride. If he is a dirt-biking nut, ask him to spend an afternoon showing you how to land a jump (just be sure to wear knee pads).

One thing to keep in mind when teaching and being taught: Patience and humility are essential. While you might not rock the house your first time at the batting cages, it's important not to let strikeouts put you in a foul mood.

The Perk: Sharing passions and picking up a new skill.

Perfect for: The adventurist.

2. Get Your Game On

It's often said that the couple that plays together stays together. Put the adage to the test by framing your first date around some friendly competition. Arranging a night of bowling, a jaunt to the mini-golf course, or a trip to the local fun zone for old-school video games and ski ball is a great way to spend quality time and get some playful physical contact going. Friendly competition is also great if you're double-dating. Try setting up a poker night or going out for laser tag—and be sure you and your guy are on the same team.

The Perk: Pressure-free physical flirting. Twister anyone?

Perfect for: Interactive or sporty types who don't take themselves too seriously.

3. Be in Pictures

If your crush is a filmmaker type, try wooing him with an artistic plan. Getting creative on a date doesn't have to mean a trip to one of those boring make-a-plate ceramic studios. Instead, ask him to shoot and edit a piece for YouTube with you. Or try taking a couple of disposable cameras out on a walk around town. Develop the film while you grab a bite to eat, or switch memory cards and agree to share pictures the next time you meet up.

The Perk: An exclusive peek into the window of his soul.

Perfect for: The photo artist.

4. Get the Ticket

Whether you're into music, theater, or underground sports, a great way to score creative points is to buy tickets to a special event. If your favorite coffeehouse is hosting an open mic or an up-and-coming comedian is performing soon, score tickets a few days in advance. (And be sure to flash your student ID since lots of places offer student discounts.) If you and your guy share a love of hip-hop and you hear of an upcoming DJ battle, jump on the opportunity to show him the greatest unknown talents.

The Perk: Showing your guy you're on the edge of cool culture.

Perfect for: The trendsetter.

You vs. the People Who (Try to) Run Your Life:

Surefire Strategies for Winning Parental Approval

4

Operation Green Light

Getting permission for a date can be a cakewalk or a full-fledged battle, depending on what your parents are like. If you're working with Mr. and Mrs. Laid-Back USA, you may already be used to setting your own rules. (If that's you, take a second to thank your lucky stars.) For the girl who practically has to give her 'rents an Excel spreadsheet filled with her afternoon plans and contacts before leaving the house, getting permission for a date may seem about as likely as becoming the next president.

But fret not. You just need to get your parents to see you in a more sophisticated, date-ready light, and all it takes is some persuasiveness and a strong case.

Planning Your Day in Court

When lobbying for what you want, approach is everything. The trick to turning your discerning dad into a personal yes-man is to plan a precise presentation, the same way a lawyer would prep a case for court.

But before you present your case, it's important to find an unobtrusive time to talk to the 'rents. You want to pick a time when they can give you their undivided attention. (Hint: If they're taming your spazzed-out brother while prepping dinner, wait.) It's also smart to pick a time when they're relaxed, like after a workout. Studies have proven that the release of endorphins that occurs during exercise elevates moods — and you want them in an elevated mood. This will ensure they are calm and not reactive, and won't make hasty decisions based on their own high stress levels. If your parents are NEVER mellow, try to schedule a talk time, so at the very least they will be able to focus on what you have to say.

THE WRONG WAY

You: Hey, Dad, I was wondering if I could go out Friday?

Dad: Can you pass that glue stick and dig up a stamp for me? I've got six minutes to get this contract to the post office.

Abort mission and try again when he's less frazzled.

THE RIGHT WAY

You: Hey, Dad, how's it going?

Dad: Pretty good. Your mother's playing tennis with the neighbor lady, and I'm about to sneak myself a hot-fudge sundae. (Wink, wink.)

Seize the day and offer to pour the chocolate sauce.

When you've got your parents' attention, start your opening argument. Tell them that you'd like to go out with a new guy, and that you're about to provide plenty of evidence as to why your unsupervised outing is a safe, fantastic, and parent-friendly idea.

Exhibit A: The Profile

Unlike the judges in our legal system, your parents might see your date as guilty until proven innocent. If your dad knows nothing about your mystery guy or your mom is convinced that this basketball player is also a player *off* the court, you must replace their delusional anxieties with a sense of security. Thus, it's time to present Exhibit A: The facts about your guy.

Tell them a little about who he is — what amps him in life, his favorite subject in school, or anything that will put a friendly, human face on what your parents see as that monster beast-child who wants to take their daughter out.

The more positive attributes you share about your guy, the better your parents will feel they know him and the higher the chance that they'll approve of your date. Of course, you don't have to spill *everything*. You might want to leave out the fact that he idolizes Marilyn Manson or is late for homeroom every day. But by throwing the 'rents a few bones about his basic vitals, you're sure to minimize the chance of their having a beef with you going out.

THE WRONG WAY

Mom, this guy is sooo cool. He's interning at West Coast Choppers, and he's got his own tattoo gun.

THE RIGHT WAY

Mom, this guy is sooo cool. He already has an internship learning mechanics and makes time to work on his artwork everyday.

Exhibit B: Sharing Your Intentions and Statute of Limitations

Now that you've eased your parents' minds by detailing what this boy is like, you can wow them with Exhibit B: your self-designed statute of limitations. This bit of evidence includes sharing whatever intentions you have for your date and breaking down the logistics (who, what, when, where). Yes, it's info they'll probably ask for any-way—but by offering it up before they have the chance to ask, you'll show your unsuspecting parents that you're taking a proactive approach in considering safety—a very adult move that will score you major points.

Say you've decided you already know homeboy pretty well, but the two of you haven't gotten the chance to kick it one-on-one. You've set your expectations for your date at getting to know him better and perhaps kissing if it feels right—but you KNOW you want to keep things PG until you've been out with him a few times. Relay that info to your parents. (How physical you want to get is a good thing for you to be thinking about regardless. There's more on this in the next chapter.)

If talking to your parents about swapping saliva with your dude is just too weird, go ahead and switch up the gory details for more general terms to convey your stance. The point is, you want to make your parents feel comfortable with your choices by showing them you've had the foresight to consider reasonable limits for your date. Warning: Many times, the 'rents can counter with the old, "I trust you, I just don't trust him." Present safety details. Tell them how you will have friends with you on your date and/or only hang out with him in public places. Promise to designate check-in times with them if they think that will be helpful. This sophisticated tactic will nip any parental paranoia in the bud and get them to genuinely consider your proposition.

THE WRONG WAY

Dad: I don't trust this bum.

You: Don't worry, Dad. He has plenty of experience and knows what he's doing.

Dad: Exactly my point. You want to end up pregnant?

You: What I want is *you* off my case! What-ever. I'm going out with this guy whether you let me or not.

Dad: Not only are you not going out with this guy, you're not leaving the house all weekend, missy!

Mission *so* not accomplished.

THE RIGHT WAY

Dad: I don't trust this bum.

You: Dad, he's not a bum. He takes AP classes and lives in his parents' house just like me. He just wants to take me to a concert.

Dad: I was a junior once. I know what this guy *really* wants.

You: You didn't raise me to be easily pressured. Plus, we are going to be in a public place the whole time.

Dad: Be home by 11 or it'll be the last first date you'll ever have.

Score!

Exhibit C: Lay Down the Law

Finally, recommend your own rules for the date. Tell them what time you think you should come home and suggest when or with whom you should check in. You may be tempted to go big on your date — in your world, a 3 am curfew, a check-in call with your party-girl BFF, and a motorcycle ride with your dude may be perfectly legit. But wake up, sister. It's crucial to make your rules realistic and in sync with what your parents might impose. The goal is to greenlight your date, and that may take some — or a lot of — compromise.

THE WRONG WAY

You: I'm going out with Joe on Saturday night.

Mom: Who's Joe?

You: Some guy.

Mom: Where are you going?

You: I just told you. OUT!

Mom: And when do you think you'll get back IN?

You: Like 2 or 3 — whenever the club closes.

Mom: There's no way. End of discussion.

THE RIGHT WAY

You: So I was thinking that Joe and I might cruise to the fair and hang on Saturday night.

Mom: Who's Joe?

You: This guy from the skate park. Janey's going, too. I'll text you after we get there to let you know everything is OK.

Mom: Well, okaaaay ...

You: If I come home around 10:30 or 11, is that cool with you?

Mom: Make it 10:30.

You: Sweet. Thanks, Mom!

If you think you should be home at midnight, but you know your parents would probably set an earlier curfew themselves, err on the side of what most closely matches your parents' style and perspective. If they're still giving cock-eyed looks, even when you suggest what you think is a reasonable curfew, ask them to chime in and negotiate. It might be annoying to set an earlier-than-desired curfew at first, but after you prove your ability to set rules and see them through, you'll be primed to establish later curfews with your parents down the road.

Though you should be ready for a courtroom-like battle, remember this is a civil negotiation — not the trial of the century. Your parents might have some outlandish ideas, but be sure to stay calm and keep your voice at a conversational tone. Listen to their viewpoints and allow them to meet your date before you go out — it's a popular request that can't always be sidestepped.

Rules for New Romance

✳ Going Offline ✳

This should go without saying, but never meet in private with someone you met online. People on the Internet may lie, and they can also be total lunatics. A group outing is the best way to meet your online interest — you'll have the support of your friends if the guy turns out to be a real-life wacko or just someone who wants more than "deep conversation over a cup of tea."

5

Date Expectations:

Writing a Dating Contract and Spotting Red Flags

Giving Yourself Guidelines

Your parents can be a royal pain at times, but they can also be right: Their radar for safety is as finely tuned as your radar for a good time.

Made-for-TV movies, magazine articles, and sex-ed courses have long been steeped in the cautionary plotlines of boy charms girl, boy corrals girl into something she doesn't want to do, and girl is emotionally scarred. It's a simple formula that has become teenage lore for a reason: It happens more often than you think.

You may consider yourself far too strong to be *that* girl, but unforeseen situations often arise on first dates that could find you unprepared and reacting in a way you wouldn't otherwise. To avoid perpetuating the girl-as-victim cliché, develop a contract for yourself that consists of rules and parameters to keep you and a new boy in check while you're out.

In your contract, which you'll draw up in the pages at the end of this chapter, you'll establish *why* you want to go out with the new guy, *how* you want to be treated, and *what* your physical boundaries are for your date.

Recognize Your Motive

First, you need to examine why you want to go out with this guy (aside from off-the-charts hotness, of course). Most first dates evolve because you want to get to know some guy better — maybe you love his laid-back style or sharp sense of humor in class, but you don't really know what he's like one-on-one.

If, however, your motives for going out with him are to make someone else jealous or to parade him around as hot property, reconsider your plan. If an ego boost is reason number one, that's something that should be achieved on your own — dating for ulterior motives is bound to hurt feelings and ruin your rep.

Set Your Terms for Treatment

Next, establish how you believe you should be treated by your new guy. We're not talking about dinner at a fancy restaurant or flowers (although those things are certainly nice). We're talking about the non-negotiable elements of respect, courtesy, and honor.

Ideally, he should:

1. listen when you have something to say and not shoot down your ideas and suggestions.

2. be physically affectionate — but not TOO much.

3. communicate with you directly and compassionately.

4. be flexible when it comes to changing plans.

5. respect your boundaries and not push you to do or talk about things you don't want to.

By identifying how you need to be treated, you are not only setting standards for yourself, but also putting these needs in the forefront of your mind. Now, if the boy fails to meet your standards while out on your date, you are more likely to recognize it when it happens instead of after the fact, and stand up for yourself (or get out of there) if need be.

RULES for New ROMANCE

✳ Get a Going Out Check-In ✳

Before you go, establish an emergency contact person who will be available to help you if things become sketchy while on your date. Pick a friend or family member who can call to check in at a designated time and is able to pick you up somewhere if necessary.

Establish Your Physical Boundaries

Remember when you presented your statute of limitations to your parents? This part of your contract will help solidify those limitations and prepare you to stick with them. To do so, take a moment to identify your intent for your date, physically speaking. What level of intimacy do you want to reach with this particular guy? Perhaps your intent is to engage in some mild make-out sessions if you both feel so inclined, but to keep the action at second base. Maybe you don't even want to kiss him until you get to know him better. (If you hardly know your date, you may want to learn more about him before you kick down some lovin'.)

It's easy to get carried away when things get hot and heavy, or to give in to his needs without considering or acting on your own. But establishing some personal boundaries ahead of time — when your mind is still clear — will help you stay grounded and keep your dignity when in the moment. His and your intentions may not perfectly align in this category, but if he is serving your needs by respecting your decisions, any difference in intents shouldn't pose a problem.

Writing Your Contract

Use the contract on the opposite page to map out your expectations and boundaries for your next first date. (Yes, contractual hearts and doodles are welcome.) Since you'll feel differently about different guys, and about yourself as you get older, take time to establish these guidelines every time you see someone new. Doing so will help keep things in control and on a positive track.

While out, pay attention to whether your needs are being met. If they're not, be your own advocate and do what you have to do to set things right. Finally, use your contract as a guideline for treating your dude with the same levels of respect, compassion, and consideration that you demand for yourself. (Remember, it's not ALL about you.)

My Personal Dating Contract	
Date:	
Dude:	
My Motive (why you want to go out with this guy)	
My Terms of Treatment (the rules of respect that outline how you should be treated)	
My Physical Boundaries (the boundaries you set for physical contact with your new guy)	
Signed:	

Red Flag!

Everyone's got a different taste in guys. Some girls favor the pretty boy or the mystery man. Or maybe you're into the math geek or school jock. But *no one* likes a flat-out jerk. Now that you've considered how you want to be treated, watch for these warning signs — they'll help you avoid those guys your mama may, or may not have, warned you about.

1

He's much, much older than you.

Some girls can't resist the charms of an older man and, because the ladies tend to mature a bit faster, a guy who's a couple of years older can make for a perfect match. But when that guy is in his twenties and the girl is in her teens, there's cause for suspicion. A much older guy has different goals and objectives when hanging with a girl — and they usually involve sex. Some guys might think it's easier to date a 15-year-old because she's potentially easier to manipulate. Letting them prove they're right is the dumbest move a smart girl can make.

2

He doesn't follow through with what he says he's going to do.

If he's late picking you up or doesn't call when he says he will, it's likely that his tendency to be thoughtless will become only more apparent as he becomes more comfortable with you.

3

He refuses to meet your parents.

Yes, meeting the parents can be a drag—especially for the shy guy—but it often needs to be done. If he refuses, he may just be nervous, in which case he might need a little coaxing. But if he absolutely won't budge, he may be seeking anonymity—a shady move that makes him come up short on the trust-o-meter.

4

He always puts himself first.

Whether it's when walking through a door or deciding what movie the two of you will see, it's important that he sometimes puts you first and considers your feelings. If he's too consumed with "me, me, me," how can he grow to care about you?

5

He arrives for your date unprepared.

You get to your destination and — surprise — he doesn't have his wallet. What's more, he isn't embarrassed about it, and expects you to pick up the slack. Free-loader alert! You may be one hot mama, but a sugar mama you're not. We all try to put our best foot forward when making first impressions. But if he is counting on you to front him money now, it's likely he'll continue to depend on you for a free ride.

6

He makes an off-color remark that's sooo out of left field.

Before reacting to his dumb comment, take a minute to breathe. Then calmly ask him to follow up or clarify. It's possible that his comment was misunderstood — poorly executed sarcasm can be a tricky thing. But if he really was being a sexist/racist/homophobe/whatever, let him know that what he said is uncool. Then consider yourself warned: This is part of his personality, and it's probably not going to change.

7

He doesn't know how to control his anger.

Everyone gets frustrated, but things can become more than unpleasant when your date takes his frustrations out on everything around him. When he yells at the theater's ticket taker, succumbs to road rage, or tosses his cell phone at a wall, you might be tempted to reason that it's OK, since he's not directing his anger at you. Stop right there. Eventually, he's bound to start throwing his rage your way. Your parents yell at you enough, do you really need to take heat from someone else?

8

He puts you in danger.

Whether he's driving like a Nascar wannabe or getting wasted at a party you've attended together, reckless behavior can not only kill your fun, it could potentially kill you. If you feel uncomfortable with any situation during your date, voice your concern. If he's clearheaded, he may respect your wishes and change his behavior. Don't be afraid of looking like a prude or nerd. You've got to stick up for yourself in a dangerous situation.

If you think he's unable to respond to your needs, call your emergency contact (p.62)—that friend or relative you prearranged to help you out if things got shady—and have them pick you up. When they arrive, calmly tell your date you've decided to head home. Though your emotions will run rampant, avoid name-calling and scene-making—they'll only escalate the situation.

6

Lights, Wardrobe ... Action!

Creating the Perfect Look for Your Date

Close Encounters (With Your Closet)

So you've nailed a date with the boy who makes your insides jump (in a good way, of course). Time for the million-dollar question: What are you going to *wear*? The goal is to come up with a kickin' outfit you feel comfortable enough to kick it in. You don't have cash to blow on a new look, and when you check your closet, all you see are last year's played-out threads. You know there's got to be something in there that makes your butt look good. If only there were a GPS device to help navigate your wardrobe.

Don't sweat it. You don't need new clothes — you need a new way of looking at the ones you already have. A few days before your date, book a private consultation with your wardrobe. It's time to reacquaint yourself with what lurks beyond the first few hangers in your closet.

Dress to Reflect

It's true what they say about first impressions. Although your guy may have seen you plenty of times before, the first time he peeps you on your date WILL leave an impact. Now ask yourself: What message do you want to send with your look?

Maybe you want to appear approachable and cute. Try denim and light makeup. If you want to show that you're active and ready for anything, rock some fly kicks and a fitted tank. How you dress not only shows what kind of girl you are, but also sets the tone for the whole evening. If you're decked out in a pencil skirt and heels, your date's probably not going to suggest batting cages and mini-golf — and if you're not exactly Sporty Spice, that might be a good thing. Here are some ideas to help you dress to reflect yourself and the kind of date you want.

Creative/Artsy

Because: You won't give up your craft-ernoon session for just anyone.

Think: Molly Ringwald in *Pretty in Pink*

The Blueprint: An asymmetrical dress, funky shoes, and a DIY handbag you just whipped up

Sporty/Active

Because: You need a guy who can handle a good a**-whooping at HORSE.

Think: Kiera Knightly in *Bend It Like Beckham*

The Blueprint: A ribbed tank, a skirt over pants, and slip on Vans — or anything cute you can move in

Boho

Because: You have to know where he stands on ethanol versus biodiesel.

Think: Kate Hudson in *Almost Famous*

The Blueprint: Knits with beaded accents and a laid-back flowy skirt

Rocker

Because: You'd rather see a live band at a loud venue than chat it up in a coffeehouse.

Think: Mary-Kate Olsen in *New York Minute*

The Blueprint: An ironic tee, distressed jeans, leather belt with studs, and kohl-rimmed eyes

Fun and Flirty

Because: Who doesn't want to get an Icee brain freeze while watching the latest Will Ferrell movie?

Think: Hilary Duff in, well, any of her flicks

The Blueprint: A clingy wrap sweater, miniskirt, and ballet flats

Classic/Ladylike

Because: A sit-down dinner and deep conversation is the perfect way to get to know someone.

Think: Jackie O.

The Blueprint: A polo shirt, bubble skirt, and kitten heels

Play With Your Clothes

Now that you know the kind of message you want to send with your outfit, it's time to get cracking in that closet. Throw some inspiring tunes on your music player, clear your bed, turn off your phone (OK, put it on vibrate), and open your mind. When looking for something to wear, *nothing* is off-limits.

1. The obvious choices will include the gear you've got in heavy rotation — meaning those threads you wouldn't be caught dead without, like your perfectly distressed jeans or new hobo bag. Pull them from your closet — or dirty clothes pile (as long as they're not completely rank) — and lay them out on your bed.

2. Scan the rest of your hanging clothes—ALL of them—and pull anything you think might work with what you've got on the bed. If there's something that catches your eye, but you're not sure it's going to work, pull it anyway. The point here is to experiment. If the color combination is enough to make you wretch, you can always take it off and erase the outfit from your memory. No one is going to see you trying on clothes in your bedroom—unless you forget to shut your blinds.

3. Do the same with the clothes in your dresser. Don't be afraid to reacquaint yourself with that long-lost crocheted top from a few years ago. It might look great over that new skull-and-bones print thermal. And don't leave out your undie drawer: The right camisole can turn a somewhat revealing shirt into a classy one.

4. After you've laid all possible options on your bed, try them on and mix 'em up. Break your own style rules. If you never wear boots with short skirts, try them together—the results might surprise you.

5. If something looked cute on the hanger but doesn't feel right when you put it on, toss it back in the closet. (Or better, make your mama proud and hang it back up.) It's best to get it out of sight so you don't confuse yourself by

trying it on again later. If one piece is cute but not working with anything you have on your bed, ditch that, too.

6. Be sure to check yourself in the mirror from all angles.
Miniskirts are fun, but you should leave something to the
imagination. If the skirt doesn't cover your butt while
sitting in a chair, consider leggings — or a longer skirt.

7. Whittle your choices down to a few outfits and keep them
out. Find shoes, jackets, and accessories that will work
for the looks that made the final cut. Now, you have three
outfits to choose from on the day of your date. That gives
you some flexibility — the winner will depend on your
mood at the time.

8. Pat yourself on the back. (But don't get your shirt dirty.)
And give yourself bonus points if you were able to con-
vince your parents you were working on homework the
entire time.

Test-Drive Your Style

Oh, the dreaded wardrobe malfunction. The wrap skirt that unwrapped itself in the wind. The undies that crept up from your low-rise jeans. And, well, there's also the Janet Jackson boob exposure that took place at Super Bowl XXX-VIII in front of millions of TV viewers. What may look flawless while you are standing still in front of a mirror could prove mortifying in action — and the last place you want to have a slip of the slip (or worse) is mid-date. What you need to do is take your preselected outfits for a little spin.

Before you go out, wear your possible date outfits while chillin' in your room. Consider the following factors: Does your shirt sag too low when you sit down and lean forward? Will your mini show London and France to the person climbing stairs behind you? Can you do a jumping jack and still keep your clothes — and boobs — in place? You may feel goofy going though this charade, but running, jumping, reaching, and bending will help you determine if your outfit is date-ready or an embarrassment waiting to happen. It will also help you burn a few calories in the interim.

Still not sure if you're working the outfit or if the outfit is working you? Get a second opinion. Your mom or that brutally honest best friend will help you sort out any doubts.

Rules for *New* Romance

✳ Know When to Fold 'Em ✳

Don't pull a Lohan, Britney, or Paris and flash
parts to your date that you wouldn't show your best
friend. When exiting a car while wearing a skirt,
keep your legs together and swing them out of the
car, then step out.

Looking Fly on the Fly

Out of nowhere, your new crush asks you to meet him at the mall! In an hour! And it takes nearly 30 minutes to get there! "Sure," you tell him coolly. You're resourceful and spontaneous. Plus, you have already used the following strategy to prepare for a last-minute date.

A color story is a group of complementary colors—about three or four. Each group creates a theme that holds together a bedroom, a bathroom, or a line of clothing. Fashion gurus use color stories all the time to build outfits, and now you will, too.

To build your own color story, pick three of the most popular colors in your wardrobe that complement each other. Here are some examples:

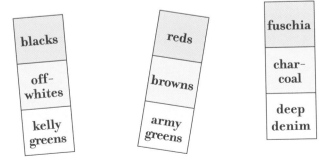

Write down your color story:

color 1:	color 2:	color 3:
_____	_____	_____

Pull all your clothes within this color story from your wardrobe and spread them on your bed.

Rank your five favorite pieces (1 is the highest).

1. _____

2. _____

3. _____

4. _____

5. _____

List your five favorite basics (these are your most versatile, perfectly fitting pieces—like your fave jeans, a white tee, or timeless peacoat).

1. _____

2. _____

3. _____

4. _____

5. _____

List accessories and shoes that match the color story you've chosen.

1. _____

2. _____

3. _____

4. _____

5. _____

Coordinate them to make three complete outfits. Then, test-drive them to make sure they work.

Next time you need a cute, last-minute ensemble, reach for one of the outfits you predesigned (Febreze it if necessary), and head out the door.

Readying Your Bod, Your Bag, and Your Brain:

7

Recipes for Panic-Free Prepping

Last-Minute Primping

Theoretically, the hour or two before your date should be relatively chill. You've cleared the major hurdles by winning battles with your parents and your closet. All that's left to do is get ready.

At this point, getting dressed might seem like a no-brainer. After all, you've already put together a foolproof outfit, so how hard can it be to slip it on? But in the hour before you leave, problems can seemingly spring up from nowhere — your hair suddenly defies all rules of physics, your closet swallowed your left boot, and the clock seems to be ticking at double time. Here are five tricks to avoid getting caught in a last-minute frenzy.

1. Do Keep It Simple

Now is not the time to be experimental. Some of the greatest looks of all time (like Mia Farrow's famous pixie cut) were born of last-minute decisions, but unless you have a celebrity stylist on speed dial, it's best to try creative hairdos and bronzing techniques earlier in the game (like when you're figuring out what to wear). Unless you've test-driven a new technique in advance, stick to familiar hair and makeup strategies to keep your prep time manageable and reduce stress.

2. Don't Get Caught Wet

Those who say they do their best thinking in the bath are on to something. Hot steamy water, time away from the bizzaro family, and visual blockage from clothes, makeup, phone, books, and life can create the perfect environment for self-reflection, daydreaming, and even singing. It's also a huge time zapper. You may have unlocked the key to the universe while soaking in the tub, but you've also lost track of the time and are suddenly 45 minutes late. The deep thoughts can wait—save yourself the stress by taking a quick shower. (Set a 10-minute timer if you have to.) You'll be happy to have more time to prep on dry land.

3. Do Keep a Steady Pace

If a normally quick-and-simple task is becoming difficult and taking more than a quarter of your allotted prep time (your normally flawless cat-eye painting skills seem to have vanished, or your updo looks like an updon't), the worst thing to do is fixate on it. Trying to make something unworkable work will suck your time like back-to-back episodes of your favorite reality show.

Instead, think of alternative solutions to your problem. There are workarounds for nearly every styling trick in the book. Just keep an open mind and be willing to adjust your look.

4. Don't Perform Major Treatments

Trying to cut, dye, or wax hair right before a date can prove disastrous. Ditto for doing facials or other dermal treatments. It usually takes about a week or so to settle into a Gwen-inspired bleach job and even longer for skin to mellow after messing with it. The last thing you need to worry about is whether your date is staring excessively at your new asymmetrical bob. (And honey, if he is, he might be a little bit gay.) To prevent last-minute styling freak-outs, be sure to take care of any facials, haircuts, and other beautifying treatments well in advance.

5. Do Be Happy With What You've Got

Despite the little disasters that may have arisen during your grooming routine, it's important to keep a big picture state of mind. Before you leave, remind yourself of your hotness and carry that attitude with you throughout your date. Your guy is obviously into you regardless of how you wear your hair, or he wouldn't be heading out with you in the first place. If the stars align for a perfect coif, consider yourself blessed. Otherwise, work what you've got — confidence beats out even the best of blowouts.

It's in the Bag

Now it's time to prep your handbag. Run through this quick checklist before you go to ensure you have everything you need to stay fresh, comfortable, and safe while you're out. Make sure your bag can easily hold all the stuff you bring — a bulging purse is a definite precursor to a makeup explosion.

- **A charged cell phone set to vibrate.** While it's impor- tant to keep your phone on, nothing kills a mood like a super loud disco beat blaring from your cellie.

- **Cash.** Bring enough to cover yourself for any activities you do. Chances are he will pick up the tab, but assuming as much can only create uncomfortable situations.

- **More cash.** You should have enough for emergency cab fare, if need be.

- **Lip gloss and other touch-up tools.** But keep it light — you'll end up with the unsightly Tammy Faye Baker effect if you keep layering makeup on through- out the night.

⚕ **A safety pin or sticky tape.** These take up virtually no space in your bag and come in handy for wardrobe malfunctions, especially at formal events.

⚕ **Mints or gum.** Like we have to tell you why.

⚕ **Keys.**

⚕ **A little something to share with your date.** This could be anything from your favorite Japanese candies (to split during the movie) to videos stored on your iPod (to watch while in line).

RULES for New ROMANCE

✳ Keep Your Engine Clean ✳

Watch what you consume before (and during) your date. If you're hoping for some smooching, avoid smoking, coffee, and sugary drinks—the breath they leave you with can be a real turnoff. What's more, guilty pleasures like caffeine, sugar, and nicotine can make you anxious and even a little spastic when they kick in.

First Date State of Mind

Ever notice that nerves can turn an otherwise charming you into a hyperactive chatter chick, a nervous miss fidget, or la femme struck suddenly mute? On a first date, these temporary personality takeovers can't always be completely prevented — butterflies in your stomach can go straight to your head. But to help channel Grace Kelly rather than Lady Insta-Clutz, you can develop a ritual to ready your mind.

To do this, factor an additional 10 to 20 minutes into your getting-ready routine to find Zen and muster mojo. What you do with this time depends on how you feel before your date (which depends on who your date is, how high your energy level is, and how long you've been battling the world's most unruly curls).

If your date follows work or an exhaustive screamfest with your older brother, a power nap — or a shot of Red Bull — might counter fatigue and get you in the groove. If your brain is speeding through the consumed-with-the-boy expressway, a good distraction, like watching YouTube clips or talking to a friend, might be the e-brake it needs. The idea is to stabilize any energy imbalance and bring yourself to a relaxed state so the natural you can shine through. Navigate the flowchart on the next page to balance out your energy and find some pre-date Zen.

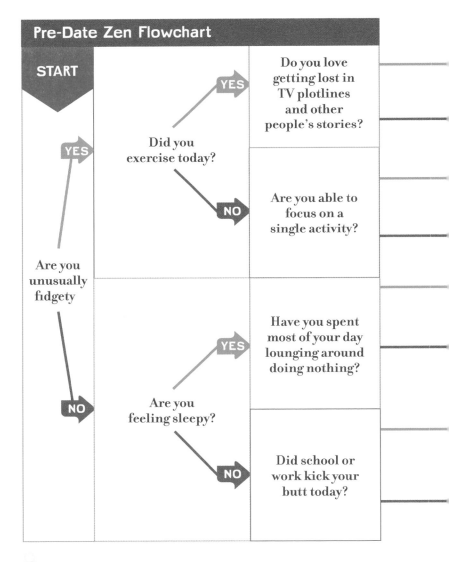

Pre-Date Zen Flowchart

START

YES

Did you exercise today?

YES — Do you love getting lost in TV plotlines and other people's stories?

NO — Are you able to focus on a single activity?

Are you unusually fidgety

NO

Are you feeling sleepy?

YES — Have you spent most of your day lounging around doing nothing?

NO — Did school or work kick your butt today?

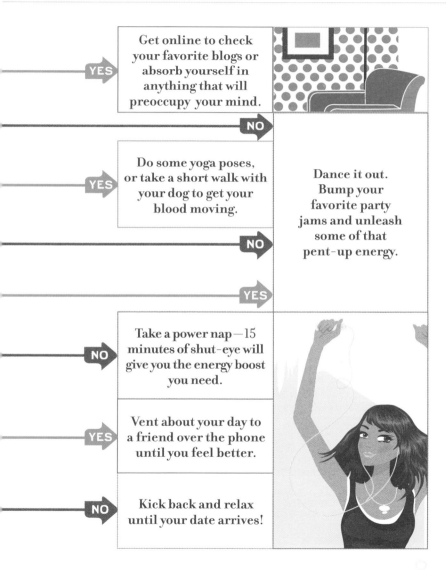

YES
Get online to check your favorite blogs or absorb yourself in anything that will preoccupy your mind.

NO

YES
Do some yoga poses, or take a short walk with your dog to get your blood moving.

NO

Dance it out. Bump your favorite party jams and unleash some of that pent-up energy.

YES

NO
Take a power nap—15 minutes of shut-eye will give you the energy boost you need.

YES
Vent about your day to a friend over the phone until you feel better.

NO
Kick back and relax until your date arrives!

8

That Did *Not* Just Happen:

Coping With Date-Related Embarrassment

Averting Disaster

In a perfect universe, you'd never get monthly cramps, schools wouldn't count absences, and every date would be Barbie-dream-world fabulous. Until then, even the most promising of dates will bring out an occasional embarrassing mishap. So what you need is an arsenal of survival tips that can help salvage your date — and your pride. Here are five I-just-want-to-hide-under-the-table first date snafus and ways to gracefully wiggle your way out of them.

1. Mortifying Parental Interaction

Sabotage upon arrival is a common form of teen torture that's been used for centuries to petrify suitors. Fortunately, some parents have evolved past the point of scaring the date, but many have not. (Picture Dad escorting your date down the hall toward his rifle collection while your sister trails them, grilling the guy about his driving skills. Ouch!) It's up to you to quickly diffuse the situation, rescue your date, and get the heck out of there as quickly as possible — without peeving your parents. Here's the plan.

First, talk to your parents beforehand about proper etiquette for dealing with your date. Reassure them that you'll invite your date in for a quick hello to keep them from freaking, but be clear about your expectations and request that they please keep extensive chattiness — and baby mug shots — out of the picture.

Second, instruct your family that NO ONE is to answer the door but you. If your family has a problem with following instructions, wait by the door 10 to 15 minutes before your date is expected to arrive, or ask him to text you when he is en route to your house. This way, you can be sure to supervise his entrance and sidestep any hostile takeovers by the family.

While running through intro-ductions, be sure to stand by his side at all times — you'll be able to guide conversations and, more important, cut them off so you don't spend half of your precious date time hanging with the 'rents. He'll also feel more secure with you nearby.

2. The Awkward Silence

It can happen to even the chattiest of Cathys: the mid-date moment of silence. Even if you've got a ton in common, the conversation well can sometimes dry up. And somehow that "sometimes" always occurs when some saccharine-loaded love ballad comes on. Ugh.

You and your date are likely to be nervous if you're out for the first time. That factor, compacted with the fact that you two have little history together, doesn't exactly pave the way for nonstop conversation. While those few talk-free moments can seem like eternities, one foolproof way to jumpstart a lagging convo is to ask your date a question about himself.

Most guys love the feeling of knowing that someone else is interested in their lives. Asking little questions, like how he spends his downtime, what movie he considers the best of the year, and even what he did last weekend can spark conversation and uncover similarities between the two of you.

When first going out with someone new, it may be best to stick with surface questions; you can delve more into hot political topics or personal matters, like why his parents got divorced, after you know each other a bit better. Keep in mind that boys aren't always as great at verbally communicating as the ladies. If he isn't the most skilled at lobbing the conversational ball back to you, keep working to guide conversations to more fun and friendly ground. After a little while together, you'll develop more of a rhythm.

3. Surprise Physical Advances

What if he unintentionally brushes your boob while reaching for the red pepper flakes at the pizza counter? Or maybe you hit his family jewels while feeling around for the popcorn bucket in his lap. The best way to reduce the embarrassment factor for these accidental run-ins is to apologize — or accept his apology — and divert attention elsewhere by keeping up the conversation.

Deflecting *intentional* physical advances can be a little tougher. If he makes a move that exceeds the boundaries you outlined in your contract of intentions, tell him you're not ready to take it there just yet, but you're having fun finding out if you can become that close in the future. Then show that you aren't one to dwell on crossed signals by taking the conversation to a more lighthearted place. If he persists, restate your stance in a more firm tone of voice and tell him that his pushy behavior is a turn off. If he won't let up, discreetly call an emergency contact person and end the date before he forces you into something you don't want.

If he's the one not ready for action, tell him that you respect his choices and are happy to take time to get to know him.

4. Accidental Innuendo and Other Foot-in-Mouth Experiences

When we're nervous or all eyes are on us, it's easy to let some stupid comment slip out of our mouths. We've all blurted out accidental double entendres and unintention-ally slanderous or insensitive comments. We often realize we've said these things the moment the words escape our lips. Immediately after the faux paux, the backpedaling kicks in, and the bad situation becomes even worse.

Take a clue from famous flubber, Jessica Simpson, who has learned over time to repair the countless social errors she makes nearly every time she opens her mouth: Acknowledge your mistake, be willing to laugh at yourself, and move on. This shows that you don't take yourself too seriously. It also opens the door for your date to loosen up. It may sound crazy but that brain fart — or actual one — may break a barrier to allow both of you to stop fronting and let your freak flags fly a bit.

5. Biological Freak-Outs

Not all mid-date meltdowns spawn from mistakes and miscalculations. Your date may be going better than imagined — but sometimes when your guy says the perfect thing or makes that sweet gesture, your face turns beet red or your stomach starts churning from excitement.

To help bring your body back to a relaxed state, excuse yourself to the restroom for a couple of deep breaths. Remind yourself that you're out for a simple good time and — if it won't ruin your makeup — cool your face and neck with a wet paper towel. When you return, you'll be set to resume as your natural, badass self with your excitability index totally in check.

9

Make Out or Make Your Escape:

How to Sweeten or Shorten Your Date

Assessing the Situation

So, now you're out. And it's great. Or maybe it's not. At some point, you'll need to decide whether to keep the ball rolling ... or make your escape.

Keep the Ball Rolling

If it's going great, you want to ensure that it stays that way. Keep these basic suggestions in mind.

1. Be a good listener.

When he's talking, give him time to complete his thought before you respond. Interrupting and talking over someone are the signatures of a yammering, self-important snot, which certainly doesn't represent the true you.

2. Remember the simple stuff.

Though it may seem painfully obvious, saying "please" and "thank you" go a long way. These little gestures are easy and thoughtful ways of acknowledging his (and others') kindness on your date.

3. Use basic table manners.

Our mothers were right again—some things never go out of style, like excusing yourself to apply lipstick, treating the server respectfully, keeping your arms off the table, and chewing quietly.

4. Express how you feel.

If you're having a good time, let him know. You don't have to blurt out "I really like you!" but a simple "Racing go-karts is such a rush. Thanks for inviting me along" lets him know you're happy and appreciative — and that should make him happy, too.

RULES for New ROMANCE

✳ Don't Pull the Meek Card ✳

Chocolate cake vs. apple pie should not be a 10-minute decision. The "whatever you want" syndrome — which can stem from the sweetest and sincerest of intentions—can quickly evolve from cute to annoying. Don't be afraid to state your preferences. It shows that you know what you like and, ultimately, reflects well on your date. You did go for him, didn't you?

Make Your Escape

Of course, despite all the fun, flirting, and exhilaration a date *can* bring, not every date is going to be completely awesome and some of them are going to downright suck.

If your date is rambling on about HIS crossbow-shooting skills, HIS killer job at the photo hut, and HIS extensive workout regimen, you may find yourself wondering, "Just where is that guy I was dying to go out with?" Nobody likes to sit through a narcissist's self-musings or to hang with someone who seems to have ordered a big ol' plate of boring for dinner.

If you realize mid-date you've landed a dud instead of a stud, the best you can do is stick it out through the remainder of your activity. Finish your dinner or whatever you're in the middle of, and then cut out after you've completed that part of the date — even if that means skipping dessert. Don't know what to say when you want to split? Here are a few escape plans to try.

1. The tired excuse.

Explain what a long day you've had and tell him you're too tired to stay out any later.

2. The stressed-out excuse.

Let him know you're having a hard time relaxing because you're worried about a big test, track meet, or whatever the next day. Tell him you think it would be best if you just went home and chilled out.

3. The emergency excuse.

Use your cell phone provider's rescue alert service or text a friend from the bathroom, and ask her to call with an "emergency." When she calls, tell him, "Something important has come up. I'm sorry, but I've got to go."

4. The truth.

And, of course, there's the novel idea of just being straight with him by saying, "I think I'm ready to go home." If you do take the high road, don't muck it up by elaborating — you're bound to say something hurtful or thwart your attempt at honesty with a lie much less believable than any of the excuses mentioned above.

RULES for
New ROMANCE

❊ Leave Yourself an Out ❊

If you are going out with a guy you don't know very well for the first time, it's wise to set up an emergency escape plan. In the beginning of your date, tell him your curfew time is earlier than it actually is. If things go well and you want to stay out with him, excuse yourself to the ladies room and, when you return, tell him you got the OK to stay out later.

10 Afterglow or Aftermath?

Getting (or Avoiding) That Second Date

Off the Hook — Your Date or Your Phone?

You've done it. Snagged a date, prepped for it like it was the SAT, and gone out with your guy. Now you're back home — feeling either blissful or blasé about the whole experience.

So what to do next?

If you'd rather undergo torture than see your date again — wasn't once torturous enough? — have mercy on him if he calls (again, it's not ALL about you). Thank him for the date, but tell him you're not interested in going out again. Of course, it's a lot easier to dodge his phone calls, but it's a cowardly move. It's also better to just nip the situation in the bud than be sent into hiding while trying to avoid him.

If you are lucky enough to feel completely enamored after your outing, wait a few days to come down from walking on clouds and phone him. Let him know how much fun you had and, if it feels right, ask him if he wants to go out again. (Or he may do the asking for you.) If a second date is arranged, start planning your outfit now.

Great Second Dates

Now that you've got that vital first date out of the way, you can plan something even better for your second. Since you've already prescreened for basic compatibility on your first date, you can devise a more unique second date that's somewhat off the beaten path.

Here are some ideas:

1. The Sunday Drive

Back when Ford's assemblymen pumped out model Ts, Americans hit the road as a relaxing way to pass time. It seems like positively forever since driving culture was about genteel exploration rather than road rage, but the serene sense of adventure from back in the day can be recaptured with a second date cruise.

Now don't get the wrong idea—driving up steep roadways to beautiful lookout points isn't all about backseat action. And a night cruise to a desolate peak probably isn't the safest choice for hanging with a guy you don't know very well. But a daytime trip that isolates you from friends, parents, and strip malls can be a perfect way to peep your community's place of natural beauty while getting to know your new sweetie better.

The Perk: Stealing alone time with your guy

Perfect for: The nature lover who can enjoy simple pleasures

2. Walk on Virgin Territory

Can you remember each time you've gone to the movies with your BFF? Run-of-the-mill outings can tend to become murky material in the memory bank. To plan an outing you and your date won't forget, arrange to do something that neither of you has done before. This could be as simple as walking the length of a local bridge, exploring an out-of-the way neighborhood, or even playing bingo at the community center. For info on upcoming and unusual events in your area (an accordion festival can make for hilarious sightseeing), check local newspapers and message boards. And don't rule out wacky activities that rate high on the ironically entertaining scale (yes, bingo). That poorly publicized monster truck rally might satisfy his appetite for destruction and your weakness for really big trucks.

The Perk: Delightfully unfamiliar sights not seen on TV

Perfect for: Those who will try anything once

3. Alphabet Dating

Have no idea what to do outside of movies and pizza? Let chance help decide. With your date, pick a letter of the alphabet, and then think of something to do that begins with that letter. If you choose B, head to a baseball game; K, a karaoke room; L, a trip to the lake for paddle boating.

The Perk: Spontaneity and great conversation fodder

Perfect for: The indecisive or fly-by-the-seat-of-your-pants kind of girl

4. Use Your Connections

For an adventure that's off the beaten path, talk to relatives, friends, and others you know about their jobs or hobbies to see what kinds of opportunities pop up. For instance, your sister's boyfriend, who leads kayak trips, might offer to guide you on an outing. And most zoo, museum, and theater employees can provide discount passes to their friends—if you ask nicely, that is. Or, if you babysit for someone who runs a paintball field or drives a cab, barter some kid-watching for free passes and rides. All it takes is a little creativity and investigation.

Rules for New Romance

✳ R–E–S–P–E–C–T ✳

On a second date, people tend to get more comfortable. But that's no excuse to abandon respect for your date, especially when it comes to personal matters. If he leaves his wallet on the table when going to the restroom, don't nose through it. If he doesn't want to talk about something, it's best to let it be. If you keep hanging out, he will open up to you about more when he's ready.

Dating Postmortem

First dates, like many things in life, are a crapshoot. Half the time, you find that you don't even like the guy you were stressing over. The other half the time, they leave you giddily re-living the experience and wanting more. Either way, recording what went down is a great way to remember your experiences—and avoid repeating outfits and outings while you're at it.

These final pages are dedicated to you, Miss Thing. Use them to rate your dates and spill any details you just can't tell your mom. You'll likely go on many first dates with new guys throughout your life (unless you get married tomorrow), and these pages will serve as an endearing and entertaining record of the amazing (and awful) romantic experiences that have shaped the dating pro you've become.

Who I Went Out With: _____

What I Wore: _____

Where We Went: _____

When: _____

My Rating: _____

The Lowdown: _____

_____

_____

Who I Went Out With: _____

What I Wore: _____

Where We Went: _____

When: _____

My Rating: _____

The Lowdown: _____

_____

_____

Who I Went Out With: _____

What I Wore: _____

Where We Went: _____

When: _____

My Rating: _____

The Lowdown: _____

_____

_____

Who I Went Out With: _____

What I Wore: _____

Where We Went: _____

When: _____

My Rating: _____

The Lowdown: _____

_____

_____

2 -2010

Erika Stalder is a San Francisco-based writer who has contributed to *Wired* and *Edutopia* magazines, and worked with the International Museum of Women to produce the *Imagining Ourselves* anthology. This is her first book.

Special Thanks To:

Alysse Aguero

Hayley Benjamin

Jamie Chambers

Mike Cossey

Alison Frenzel

Curtis Gaylor

Joe Guadarrama

Evan Kristiansen

Diane Kwan

Bob Larsen

Matt Mcguire

Megan Morrissui

Eleni Nicholas

Aphrodite Obezo

Cassandra Pena

Andie Savard

Jo Stalder